Mastering College Cooking

A Comprehensive Guide To Healthy, Budget-Friendly Recipes For Every Student To Gain Energy While Enjoying Delicious Meals

LEANNY HERO

Mastering College Cooking

Copyright & Disclaimers

Copyright 2021 LEANNY HERO. All Rights Reserved.

Post Pro Solutions

No part of this book may be reproduced without written permission from the author.

* **Author's note**: Please be aware that I am not certified Cookbook writer and I take no liability or responsibility for anything you decide to do because of the information in this book. This book is for guide cookbook recipes. purpose exclusively. It is recommended that you talk to a health professional before making any significant changes to your daily recipes or any activity levels.

TABLE OF CONTENTS

CHAPTER 1 SLOW COOKER RECIPE UNDER 300 CALORIES 8
    1. Slow Cooked Balsamic Greens 8
    2. Dark Bean and Sweet Potato Chili 10

CHAPTER 2 CHICKEN RECIPE 12
    3. Chicken with honey 12
    4. Sweet, sour chicken 13

CHAPTER 3 BREAKFAST 16
    5. Mushroom, Tomato, Basil Frittata 16
    6. Perfect Oatmeal 18
    7. Poached Egg Over Mediterranean Kale 20
    8. Poached Eggs 22
    9. Poached Eggs Over Collard Greens and Shiitake Mushrooms ... 23
    10. Poached Eggs Over Sautéed Greens 26
    11. Poached Eggs Over Spinach 28

CHAPTER 4 SALAD ENTREES 32
    12. Healthy Chef's Salad With Walnuts And French Dressing 32
    13. Healthy Chicken Caesar Salad 35
    14. Healthy Turkey Salad 37
    15. Healthy Veggie Salad 38
    16. Kidney Bean Salad With Mediterranean Dressing 40
    17. Marinated Bean Salad 42
    18. Mediterranean Baby Spinach Salad 44
    19. Mediterranean Pasta Salad 46

CHAPTER 5 SOUPS ... 48

20. Red Kidney Bean Soup With Lime Yogurt ... 48
21. Seafood Gazpacho ... 51
22. Shiitake Mushroom Seaweed Soup ... 54
23. Hot Cabbage Soup ... 56
24. Fiery Posole Soup ... 58
25. Super Energy Kale Soup ... 60
26. Turkey And Vegetable Chili Verde ... 63
27. Zesty Mexican Soup ... 65

CHAPTER 6 FISH ... 68

28. 5-Minute "Quick Broiled" Salmon ... 68
29. 5-Minute Boiled Large Shrimp ... 70
30. Baked Salmon & Walnut Patties With Red Bell Pepper Sauce 72
31. Halibut With Ginger And Scallions ... 75
32. Miso Salmon ... 77
33. Salmon With Dill Sauce ... 80
34. Salmon With Maple Dijon Glaze ... 82

CHAPTER 7 CHICKEN AND TURKEY ... 84

35. Broiled Rosemary Chicken Over Puréed Lentils And Swiss Chard 84
36. Curried Chicken Over Spinach ... 88
37. Healthy Sautéed Red Cabbage With Baked Chicken Breast 90
38. Holiday Turkey With Rice Stuffing & Gravy With Fresh Herbs 93
39. Quick Broiled Chicken Breast With Honey-Mustard Sauce 99
40. Roast Turkey Breast With Chipotle Chili Sauce ... 102
41. Sesame Braised Chicken & Cabbage ... 104

CHAPTER 8 LEAN MEAT ... 108

42. Roast Leg Of Lamb ... 108

	43. Rosemary "Quick Broiled" Lamb	110

CHAPTER 9 VEGETARIAN ENTREES 112

	44. Indian-Style Lentils	112
	45. Quick Black Bean Chili	114

CHAPTER 10 SIDE SALAD/DRESSINGS 116

	46. Great Antipasto Salad	116
	47. Kiwi Salad	118
	48. Grape And Melon Salad	119
	49. Mediterranean Tomato Salad	120
	50. Cranberry Sauce	122

CHAPTER 1
SLOW COOKER RECIPE UNDER 300 CALORIES

Many individuals in a weight reduction venture check the calories of the food they eat every day. Like this, it will be simpler for them to keep tabs on their development. In case you're attempting to shed off individual pounds yet need to appreciate home-cooked meals, draw out your simmering pot and cook these healthy moderate cooker recipes that are equivalent to 300 calories or less.

Attempt these healthy moderate cooker recipes which are useful for weight reduction:

1. Slow Cooked Balsamic Greens

What you need:

- 3 bacon cuts
- 2 cloves garlic, minced
- 1 inlet leaf
- 1 can without fat lower-sodium chicken stock

- 2 cups chopped new collard greens

- 1 cup chopped onion

- 3 tablespoons balsamic vinegar

- 1 tablespoon nectar

- 1/4 teaspoon salt

Cook bacon to a fresh in a dish over medium-high warmth. Eliminate from skillet, disintegrate and put in a safe spot. In a similar skillet with the bacon drippings, cook onion until tender, around 5 mins. Mix in collard greens and cook until tender. Spot blend in a moderate cooker alongside narrows leaf, garlic and stock. Cover and cook for 3 to 4 hours on low. Then, join balsamic vinegar and nectar in a bowl. At the point when greens are prepared, mix in balsamic blend not long before serving. Top with disintegrated bacon.

2. Dark Bean and Sweet Potato Chili

What you need:

- 3 medium sweet potatoes, cut into scaled-down pieces
- 1 white onion, diced
- 2 cups stout salsa
- 2 cups dark beans with salt
- 2 cups vegetable stock
- 2 cups of water
- 1 tablespoon vegetable oil
- Salt and pepper

Warmth vegetable oil in a dish and cook onion until tender, season with salt and pepper. Add sweet potato cuts and cook for 3 minutes. Spot blend in a moderate cooker. At that point, mix in salsa, dark beans, vegetable stock and water. Cover and cook for 3 to 4 hours on low until sweet potatoes and dark beans are tender.

Presently you don't need to stress over your weight while eating delicious food - attempt these healthy moderate cooker recipes under 300 calories!

Mastering College Cooking

CHAPTER 2
CHICKEN RECIPE

3. Chicken with honey

It takes four to six people: 600 g chicken filet, 300 g spaghetti, 100 g carrot, 50 g celery roots, stems celery 50 g, 20 g of nectar, 1 tablespoon mustard, 1/2 teaspoon pepper, 2 tablespoons oil, 2 to 3 tablespoons soy sauce, a little salt, 2 tablespoons parsley.

Preparation:

cook the chicken pieces and sprinkle with the pepper. Mustard and nectar well and mix them covering the chicken. Let the meat marinated for, in any event, two hours. Cook the vegetables for around five minutes in 300 ml boiling water. Fry marinated chicken in the hot oil. Add the cubes cut vegetables, and pour 150 ml of water. Keep on stewing in the gentle fire until the meat and vegetables are not delicate. Delicately cooked spaghetti, add the excess fluid and soy sauce, and by and by, cook it.

4. Sweet, sour chicken

- 2 kg of chicken
- 300 g lettuce
- 200 gr green beans
- celery
- carrot
- 4 tablespoons raisins
- onion
- garlic
- coriander
- cinnamon
- nutmeg
- pepper

Blend all the spices. Lastly, join them with the chopped carrot, celery, highly contrasting onions. With this blend, fill the chicken, put it in an enormous pot, add water, and cook it for 60 minutes. Could you leave it to cool? Cook the green beans in salted water; wash green salad, and lemon strip cut into slim strips. Oil, vinegar, raisins and lemon strip blend. Separate chicken from bones, cut into slight noodles and spot it on a plate with salad and green beans. Pour prepared sauce of raisins and serve.

CHAPTER 3
BREAKFAST

5. Mushroom, Tomato, Basil Frittata

Frittatas, for example, are an extraordinary expansion to your Healthiest Way of Eating any season of day. They do not just give incredible flavor one serving contains just 144 calories. Appreciate!

Prep and Cook Time: 20 minutes

Ingredients:

- 1/2 medium onion, minced
- 3 medium cloves garlic, squeezed
- 1 TBS +1 TBS chicken stock
- 1 cup daintily cut crimini mushrooms
- 1/2 medium tomato diced
- 3 enormous eggs

- 3 TBS chopped new basil

- salt and dark pepper to taste

Headings:

1. Mince onions and press garlic, and let sit for 5 minutes to bring out their concealed health benefits.

2. Warmth 1 TBS stock in a 10-inch stainless steel skillet. Healthy Sauté onion over medium-low warmth for 3 minutes, mixing as often as possible.

3. Add garlic and mushrooms and proceed to sauté for an additional 2 minutes.

4. Add 1 TBS stock, tomato, salt, and pepper and cook for one more moment. Mix well and tenderly scratch the dish with a wooden spoon to eliminate any slight consumption.

5. Beat eggs well, and season with salt and pepper. Blend in chopped basil. Pour eggs over vegetables equitably and go warmth to low. Cover and cook for around 5 minutes, or until firm. Cut into wedges and serve.

6. Perfect Oatmeal

A perfect method to begin a day of healthy eating. What's more, who might have felt that a bowl of oatmeal could give over a portion of the everyday esteem for those elusive omega-3 fatty acids!

Prep and Cook Time: 15 minutes

Ingredients:

- 2-1/4 cups water
- run salt
- 1 cup customary moved oats
- 1/2 tsp cinnamon
- 1/4 cup dried cranberries
- 1/4 cup chopped pecans
- 1 TBS ground flaxseeds
- 1 TBS blackstrap molasses
- 1 cup milk or sans dairy milk elective

Bearings:

Consolidate the water and salt in a little pan and turn the warmth to high.

When the water bubbles, turn the warmth to low, add oatmeal, and cook, blending, until the water is simply ingested, around 5 minutes. Add cinnamon, cranberries, pecans, and flaxseeds. Mix, cover the skillet, and mood killer heat. Let sit for 5 minutes. Present with milk and molasses.

7. Poached Egg Over Mediterranean Kale

Veggies are an extraordinary method to begin the day. It requires some investment to set up the kale and top with a poached or delicate bubbled egg.

Poached Egg throughout Mediterranean KalePrep and Cook Time: 5 minutes

Ingredients:

- 2 omega-3 rich eggs

- 1 lb Kale

- 1 TBS Mediterranean Dressing

- 1 TBS pumpkin seeds

Headings:

Fill the lower part of the steamer with 2 crawls of water.

While steam is developing, remove the thick stem closures and cut Kale leaves into 1/8-inch slices (thick stems can be put aside for soup). (Wavy Kale can be destroyed in a food processor.) Slicing Kale daintily guarantees in any event, cooking and the best flavor. Allow cut Kale to sit for 5-10 minutes before steaming.

Let chopped or squeezed garlic and let sit for in any event 5 minutes.

At the point when water goes to a full bubble, place kale in the steamer. Cover with a tight-fitting top and steam for 5 minutes for still somewhat firm Kale.

Move to a bowl and throw Kale with the Mediterranean Dressing and top with poached or delicate bubbled egg and pumpkin seeds.

Serves 2

Important: For best flavor, utilize a blade and fork to cut the

Cooked Kale across a few times until it is in exceptionally little pieces. The more finely you cut Kale, the more uncovered surface zone you make. This can permit more

Flavors of the dressing to pass into the Kale and accelerate attractive changes in surface, including tenderness.

Research shows that fat-solvent vitamins and carotenoids found in nourishments, for example, Kale, might be better assimilated when overcome with fat-containing food sources like additional virgin olive oil. The dressing will likewise help soften the Kale.

8. Poached Eggs

For perfect poached eggs.

Prep and Cook Time: 5 minutes

Ingredients:

- 1-2 eggs

Bearings:

Bring 2-3 inches water to a medium bubble in a sauce dish. Add 1 tsp of light vinegar, for example, wine or apple juice vinegar (use around 1/4 tsp per cup of water). Vinegar helps hold the egg whites together. Try not to add salt to the water as it disintegrates egg whites. Not long before adding the eggs, whirl the water with a spoon to make a round movement in the water. This will help keep the egg together as it cooks.

Break eggs into a little bowl each in turn and slip them into the stewing water.

Cook 5 minutes, until the white is set and the yolk has shot over. Eliminate eggs with an opened spoon and channel on paper towels.

9. Poached Eggs Over Collard Greens and Shiitake Mushrooms

This formula is an extraordinary one for supper, just like breakfast. The shiitake mushrooms add a unique umami Asian flavor to this dish.

Prep and Cook Time: 20 minutes

Ingredients:

- 6 cups chopped collard greens
- 1 medium onion, cut down the middle and cut meager
- 6 new shiitake mushrooms, cut medium-thick, stems eliminated
- 4 new omega-3-rich eggs
- around 4 cups water
- 1 TBS apple juice vinegar, or any white wine vinegar

Dressing

- 1 TBS new lemon juice
- 1 TBS minced new ginger

- 3 medium cloves garlic squeezed

- 1 TBS soy sauce

- 1 TBS additional virgin olive oil

- salt and white pepper to taste

Headings:

1. Cut onions and press garlic, and let sit for 5-10 minutes to bring out their health-promoting benefits.

2. Bring 2" of water to a bubble in a steamer pot.

3. Wash greens well. Fold or stack leaves and cut into 1/4" slices and cut again transversely. Let sit for 5-10 minutes.

4. Steam collard greens, mushrooms and onions together for 5 minutes.

5. While steaming greens, prepare for poaching eggs by bringing water and vinegar to a quick stew in a little, shallow skillet. You can begin on high warmth, and once it reaches boiling point, diminish warmth to a stew prior to adding eggs. Ensure there is sufficient water to cover eggs.

6. Combine lemon juice, ginger, garlic, soy sauce, olive oil, salt, and pepper in a little bowl.

7. Poach eggs until wanted doneness. This will take around 5 minutes, or just until the white is set and the yolk has been recorded over.

8. Eliminate vegetables from steamer and throw with dressing. Eliminate eggs from water with an opened spoon and spot on a plate of threw greens.

10. Poached Eggs Over Sautéed Greens

Appreciate vegetables for breakfast! In numerous pieces of the world, vegetables are an ordinary piece of a healthy breakfast. This Healthiest Way of the Eating dish not just tastes extraordinary, it contains just 130 calories and gives an abundance of health-promoting supplements.

Prep and Cook Time: 25 minutes

Ingredients:

- 4 eggs, ideally o

- 1 tsp light vinegar (rice, apple juice, or white wine)

- around 4 cups water

- 1 cup daintily cut leeks, around 1 enormous leek, white part as it were

- 6 medium cloves garlic, cut

- 4 cups finely chopped kale

- 3 + 5 TBS chicken stock

- 2 TBS new lemon juice

- salt and dark pepper to taste

Bearings:

Cut leeks and garlic and let sit for at any rate 5 minutes to bring out their health-promoting properties.

Bring water and vinegar to a quick stew in a skillet adequately huge to fit eggs. Ensure there is sufficient water to cover eggs.

While water is going to a stew, heat 3 TBS stock in a different stainless steel 10-12 inch skillet. Healthy Sauté cut leeks in stock over medium warmth for around 3 minutes. Add garlic slices and keep on sauting, mixing continually for one more moment.

Add kale, stock, and lemon juice, and stew covered on medium-low warmth for around 5 minutes, mixing at times.

At the point when done, prepare with salt and pepper.

Poach eggs until wanted doneness. This will take around 5 minutes, or just until the white is set and the yolk has shot over. Eliminate from vinegar water with an opened spoon and spot on top of greens.

11. Poached Eggs Over Spinach

Start the day with an additional increase in greens in this simple to-get ready supper that you can likewise serve for lunch or supper.

Prep and Cook Time: 15 minutes

Ingredients:

- 2 omega-3 advanced eggs
- 1 tsp light vinegar
- 1 lb new spinach (or kale or collard greens)
- Mediterranean Dressing
- 1 TBS additional virgin olive oil
- 1 tsp new lemon juice
- 1 medium clove garlic
- ocean salt and pepper to taste

Bearings: Spinach

1. Utilize a huge pot (3 quarts) with loads of water. Bring water to a quick bubble.

2. While water is reaching boiling point, press or hack garlic and let it sit for in any event 5 minutes to upgrade its health-promoting properties.

3. Wash spinach.

4. At the point when water is at full bubble, place spinach into the pot. Try not to cover. Cooking revealed causes the acids to escape into the air. Cook spinach for 1 moment; start timing a soon as you drop the spinach into the bubbling water. See 5-Minute Kale or 5-Minute Collard Greens plans on the off chance that you utilize these greens instead of spinach.

5. After the spinach has cooked for 1 moment (don't trust that water will re-visitation of a bubble), utilize a lattice sifter with a handle to eliminate spinach from the pot. Press out overabundance fluid.

6. Throw spinach with dressing ingredients while it is as yet hot. The mediterranean dressing doesn't need to be made independently.

Poached Eggs

Bring 1-quart water to a high stew in a 10-inch skillet with 1 tsp of vinegar.

When water goes to a high stew, poach eggs for around 5 minutes, or until whites are firm. Eliminate from the water with an opened spoon and spot over spinach combination.

Serves 2

Nutritional Profile accessible soon.

CHAPTER 4
SALAD ENTREES

12. Healthy Chef's Salad With Walnuts And French Dressing

This salad is restricted simply by your creative mind. Use it as a base, yet blend and match your favorite vegetables on the off chance that you'd preferably substitute chicken bosom for the turkey.

Prep and Cook Time: 15 minutes

Ingredients:

- 4 cups blended salad greens

- 4 oz cut turkey bosom

- 4 oz low-fat cheddar

- 1/4 cup cucumbers, cut

- 1/4 cup new ready tomato, diced

- 1/4 cup celery, diced
- 3 TBS walnuts, chopped
- 1 TBS French Dressing
- French Dressing
- 1/2 cup additional virgin olive oil
- 1 TBS onion, chopped fine
- 4-1/2 tsp red wine vinegar
- 2 tsp tomato glue
- 1 tsp mustard powder
- 2 TBS honey
- 1 tsp paprika
- 1/2 tsp celery seeds
- salt and pepper to taste

Headings: Salad

Spot greens on a plate and top with the remainder of the ingredients.

Top with the dressing.

French Dressing

In a blender, mix all ingredients, aside from olive oil and salt and pepper, until smooth.

With blender running, gradually pour in the olive oil until emulsified.

Season to taste with salt and pepper.

13. Healthy Chicken Caesar Salad

You can add or substitute any of the vegetables with your undisputed top choices or use what you have available. This is a healthy form of a Caesar salad that is just restricted by your creative mind.

Prep and Cook Time: 15 minutes

Ingredients:

- 4 cups chopped blended greens (spinach, romaine, arugula)
- 2 oz chicken or turkey slices
- 1 medium tomato, chopped or cut
- 1/4 cup cucumbers, cut
- 1/4 cup crimini mushrooms, cut
- 1 cup or 1/2 can (BPA Free) kidney beans
- 1 TBS dried sunflower seeds

Dressing

- 2 TBS new lemon juice

- 1/2 TBS additional virgin olive oil

- 1 clove garlic, pressed or chopped

- 1 TBS parmesan cheddar

Bearings:

Combine all ingredients and top with dressing.

14. Healthy Turkey Salad

This turkey salad is speedy, simple, and adaptable. Utilize whatever vegetables you have close by to make your very own variety.

Prep and Cook Time: 10 minutes

Ingredients:

- 4 cups blended greens
- 1/2 medium tomato, cut
- 3 oz turkey bosom, cut
- 1/4 cup crimini mushrooms, cut
- 3-1/2 TBS sunflower seeds
- 2/3 cup cooked kidney beans or canned (no BPA)

Bearings:

Combine all ingredients and top with our Blue Cheese Dressing.

15. Healthy Veggie Salad

A huge salad meal with veggies and beans can bring you through the whole evening. This recipe is only an example of what you can make yourself with your favorite ingredients.

Prep and Cook Time: 10 minutes

Ingredients:

- 4 cups blended salad greens

- 2 oz low-fat cheddar

- 1/2 cup cucumber slices

- 1/2 cup tomato, diced

- 1/2 cup cut red chime pepper

- 1/4 cup avocado, diced

- 1 cup garbanzo beans

- 1/2 cup crimini mushrooms

- 3 TBS sunflower seeds

Dressing

- 1 TBS additional virgin olive oil

- 1 tsp lemon juice

- salt and pepper to taste

Bearings:

Combine all ingredients. Toss with olive oil and lemon juice. Add salt and pepper to taste.

16. Kidney Bean Salad With Mediterranean Dressing

The dressing utilized in this salad is adaptable and can be utilized on a wide range of vegetables.

Prep and Cook Time: 15 minutes

Ingredients:

- 1 ear of crude corn bits
- 1/4 cup minced red onion
- 1 15oz can kidney beans, flushed and depleted
- 1 medium tomato, chopped
- 2 TBS new parsley or cilantro, minced
- Mediterranean Dressing
- 4-5 cloves garlic, chopped or pressed
- 1 cup additional virgin olive oil
- 1/3 cup new lemon juice
- ocean salt and pepper to taste

Headings:

Combine all ingredients and toss with 1/2 cup Mediterranean Dressing.

Mediterranean Dressing

Press garlic and let it sit for 5 minutes.

Whisk together the lemon juice, garlic, ocean salt, and pepper.

Gradually pour the additional virgin olive oil into the blend while whisking continually. The more gradually you pour, and the quicker you whisk, the thicker and creamier the dressing will be.

The dressing will store in the refrigerator for as long as 10 days. It will harden, so you should bring it back to room temperature prior to utilizing it.

Servings

Salad: Serves 2

Dressing: Yields around 1-1/3 cup

To add extra flavor and nutrition to the dressing, you can add any of the accompanyings: minced basil or cilantro, minced onion, curry powder, honey, finely diced avocado or red chime pepper (if utilizing avocado or ringer pepper, use dressing right away).

Alternative: Dressing ingredients can be added straightforwardly to vegetables or salads without whisking.

17.   Marinated Bean Salad

This is an extraordinary dish to add to your Healthiest Way of Eating since you can keep in your refrigerator for 3-4 days and its flavor improves every day!

Marinated Bean Salad   **Prep and Cook Time:** 25 minutes

Ingredients:

2 TBS minced onion

3 medium cloves garlic, pressed

2 cups new green beans cut into 1-inch lengths

2 cups or 1 15 oz can (sans bpa) lima beans, depleted and flushed

2 cups or 1 15 oz can (sans bpa) kidney beans, depleted and flushed

1 enormous ready new tomato, chopped

2 TBS chopped new basil (or 2 tsp dried basil)

1 TBS chopped new oregano (or 1 tsp dried oregano)

1 TBS chopped new parsley (or 1 tsp dried parsley)

3 TBS new lemon juice

2-3 TBS additional virgin olive oil

salt and broken dark pepper to taste

Bearings:

1. Mince onion and press garlic, and let sit for 5 minutes to bring out its health-promoting benefits.

2. Fill the lower part of a steamer with 2 crawls of water.

3. While steam is developing in steamer cut green beans.

Steam for 5 minutes. A fork should puncture them effectively when they are finished.

4. Channel and wash canned beans. Allow beans to sit in a colander for another couple of minutes to deplete overabundance water.

5. Combine all ingredients. If you have the opportunity, let it marinate for at any rate 15 minutes. It can keep in the refrigerator for a couple of days. Keep available for a speedy meal.

18. Mediterranean Baby Spinach Salad

Appreciate this new salad made with infant spinach for a total lunch meal. Add the ingredients we recommend, or whatever different ingredients you have available to suit your taste.

Prep and Cook Time: 10 minutes

Ingredients:

- 8 cups new infant spinach

- 1 hard bubbled egg, ideally organic, cut fifty-fifty the long way

- 6 olives

- 1/2 cup feta cheddar, disintegrated

- 1 cup entire cherry tomatoes, chopped

- 1 cup garbanzo beans

- 2 TBS red ringer pepper, cut

- 3 TBS additional virgin olive oil

- 1 TBS new lemon juice

- ocean salt and pepper to taste

Discretionary: onions, crimini mushrooms, avocado, anchovies

Headings:

Gap spinach onto two plates and top each presenting with half of the leftover ingredients.

19. Mediterranean Pasta Salad

Combine the new taste of vegetables and spices with pasta for a salad loaded with flavor and simple to plan.

Prep and Cook Time: 25 minutes

Ingredients:

- 1/4 lb fusilli (wine tool) pasta

- 1 enormous pack asparagus cut into 1-inch lengths, disposing of base fourth

- 1/2 medium onion, minced

- 1/2 container cherry tomatoes, quartered

- 5-6 medium cloves garlic, pressed

- 3 TBS chopped new basil (or 1 TBS dried basil)

- 1 TBS chopped new tarragon(or 1 tsp dried tarragon)

- 3 TBS new lemon juice

- 1 TBS balsamic vinegar

- 3 TBS additional virgin olive oil

- salt and broken dark pepper to taste

- *optional 4 oz goat cheddar

Headings:

1. Cook pasta, as indicated by guidelines on the bundle.

2. While pasta is cooking, plan the rest of the ingredients. Spot everything except for asparagus in a bowl and put it in a safe spot.

3. At the point when pasta is around a short ways from being done, add asparagus to cooking pasta. (On the off chance that asparagus is thick, you might need to add 4 minutes before it's finished. Or then again, on the off chance that it is slender, add 2 minutes before it's done.) Drain and flush in virus water in a colander when done. Ensure it depletes well, so it doesn't weaken flavor.

4. Toss with the rest of the ingredients, and season with salt and pepper.

CHAPTER 5
SOUPS

20. Red Kidney Bean Soup With Lime Yogurt

Soups are the ideal warm-up dinner. This right, fiery bean soup is an extraordinary expansion to your Healthiest Way of Eating as the days get more limited and the temperature keeps on cooling.

Prep time: 15 minutes **Cooking time:** 20 minutes

Ingredients:

- 1 medium onion, chopped
- 1 medium carrot, chopped in 1/2-inch pieces
- 1 stem celery, chopped in 1/2-inch pieces
- 4 medium cloves garlic, chopped
- 3 cups + 1 TBS chicken or vegetable stock

- 3 TBS tomato glue

- 1 TBS ground cumin

- 2 TBS red chili powder

- 1 TBS dried oregano

- 2 cups or 1 15 oz can natural red kidney beans, depleted

- salt and pepper to taste

- Lime yogurt

- 1/2 cup plain yogurt

- 1 TBS lime juice

- 1 TBS chopped new cilantro

Bearings:

Cleave onions and garlic and let sit for 5 minutes to draw out their shrouded medical advantages.

Hack carrots and celery.

Warmth 1 TBS stock in a medium-sized soup pot. Healthy Sauté onion in stock over medium warmth for around 5 minutes, mixing as often as possible, until clear. Add garlic, carrots, celery, and proceed to sauté for one more moment.

Add stock, tomato glue, kidney beans, and spices. Heat to the point of boiling. When it reaches boiling point, diminish warmth to medium-low and stew revealed for another 15-20 minutes, or until vegetables are tender. Let cool for a couple of moments while making lime yogurt.

Make lime yogurt by joining yogurt, lime juice, and cilantro in an independent little bowl.

Mix soup. Be mindful to begin blender on low speed, so hot soup doesn't emit and consume you. What's more, ensure you don't fill the blender the greater part full.

Season with salt and pepper to taste. Reheat, and fill serving bowls, top with a spoonful of lime yogurt, and serve.

21. Seafood Gazpacho

While traditional gazpacho isn't made with seafood, this special variety makes this form more nutritious and fulfilling and an extraordinary expansion to your Healthiest Way of Eating. Appreciate the additional increase in those elusive omega-3 unsaturated fats that come from both the shrimp and scallops.

Prep and Cook Time: 25 minutes

Ingredients:

- 1/2 lb straight scallops, rinsed and wiped off
- 1/4 cup new lemon juice
- 2/3 cup diced cucumber
- 1 medium yellow chime pepper, diced into 1/4-inch pieces
- 1 medium tomato, chopped, seeds and overabundance mash eliminated
- 1/2 medium onion, finely minced
- 3 medium cloves garlic, squeezed

- 4 oz can diced green chili

- 3 TBS chopped new cilantro

- 2 TBS additional virgin olive oil

- 1/4 lb little cooked shrimp, rinsed and wiped off

- 3 cups tomato juice

- salt and broken dark pepper to taste

Headings:

1. Rinse and dry scallops. Put into lemon juice.

2. Mince onion and press garlic and let sit for 5 minutes to draw out their wellbeing advancing properties

3. Prepare rest of the ingredients and blend in a bowl with onion and garlic

4. Add scallops and lemon juice at the end. Allowing the scallops to scallops in the lemon juice while planning the rest of the ingredients permits them to marinate. If you can prepare this soup early and place it in the fridge for an hour or more, the taste improves.

Serves 4

The narrows scallops are added crude to this soup. Marinating in the lemon juice cooks them marginally. In the event that you favor having them cooked more, steam for around 1 moment (watch the clock as cooking for any longer will overcook them and make them intense). You might need to salt similarly as you are serving this soup. The salt will draw out the water from the cucumber and weaken the flavor. Additionally, this soup looks and tastes best if the peppers and cucumbers are cut about a similar size as the scallops. By cutting them little, the kinds of the various ingredients mix better.

22. Shiitake Mushroom Seaweed Soup

Attempt this delicious blend of seaweed and shiitake mushrooms to add an increase in minerals, particularly iodine, to your Healthiest Way of Eating. Appreciate!

Prep and Cook Time: 30 minutes

Ingredients:

- 6 entire dried medium shiitake mushrooms
- 6 cups warm water
- 4 medium-sized pieces of wakame seaweed
- 1 medium onion, quartered and cut flimsy
- 3 medium cloves garlic, chopped
- 2 TBS minced new ginger
- 2 TBS dry vegetable stock powder
- 2 TBS chopped dulse seaweed
- 2 TBS soy sauce
- 1 TBS rice vinegar
- 3 TBS minced scallion greens for garnish

- salt and white pepper to taste

Headings:

Rinse mushrooms and wakame and absorb 2 cups of warm water for around 10 minutes, or until delicate. Save water.

Warmth 1 TBS mushroom-seaweed water in medium-sized soup pot. Add onion and Healthy Sauté over medium warmth for around 5 minutes blending every now and again. Add garlic and ginger and proceed to sauté for one more moment.

At the point when mushrooms and wakame are delicate, cut the mushrooms slim and hack the seaweed. Cut out stems when cutting mushrooms and dispose of them. Add to soup pot alongside drenching water, and 4 additional cups of water and dry vegetable stock. Heat to the point of boiling on high warmth.

Add dulse.

When it re-visitations of a bubble, lessen warmth to medium and stew revealed for around 10 minutes. Season with soy sauce, rice vinegar, salt, and pepper. Add minced scallion and serve.

Serves 4

Serve with Chinese Cabbage Salad

23.   Hot Cabbage Soup

The uncommon blend of cabbage and vegetables in this healthy soup is united flawlessly with the spices. The Healthy Sauté cooking strategy makes it light and more beneficial without heating oils or bargaining flavor.

Prep and Cook Time: 45 minutes

Ingredients:

- 1 medium onion, quartered and cut flimsy
- 3 medium cloves garlic, chopped
- 1-2 tsp minced new chili pepper (serrano or jalapeno)
- 2 tsp ground coriander
- 1 TBS dry mustard
- 5 cups + 1 TBS chicken or vegetable stock
- 2 TBS new lemon juice
- 2 medium-sized red potatoes cut in 1/2-inch blocks (around two cups)

- 1 15 oz can diced tomatoes

- 3 cups meagerly cut Savoy or green cabbage

- salt and dark pepper to taste

Headings:

Warmth 1 TBS stock in a medium soup pot. Healthy Sauté cut onion over medium warmth for around 5 minutes. Mix in garlic and minced chili pepper. Keep on sauting for one more moment.

Mix in dried coriander and mustard. Add stock and the remainder of ingredients aside from the cabbage, salt, and pepper. Stew for around 20 minutes, revealed, or until potatoes are tender.

Add cabbage, and cook for an additional 5 minutes. Season with salt and pepper to taste.

24. Fiery Posole Soup

Join this simple-to-prepare soup with an enormous salad for a quick bite that tastes extraordinary as well as will fulfill your craving. If you can't discover hominy in the canned vegetable part of your supermarket, look in the segment that highlights Spanish/Mexican foods.

Prep and Cook Time: Prep time: 15 minutes Cooking time: 20 minutes

- **Ingredients:**

- 1 medium onion, chopped

- 6 medium cloves garlic, chopped

- 4 cups + 1 TBS chicken or vegetable stock

- 2 TBS new lime juice

- 3 cups kale, rinsed and chopped fine

- 2 cups canned hominy, depleted

- 15 oz can diced tomatoes

- 4 oz can dice green chili

- 3 TBS chopped new cilantro

- salt and pepper to taste

Bearings:

1. Hack onion and garlic and let sit for 5 minutes before cooking to draw out their shrouded medical advantages.

2. Rinse kale and eliminate stems. Cleave fine.

3. Warmth 1 TBS stock in the medium-sized soup pot. Healthy Sauté onion in stock over medium warmth for 5 minutes blending now and again, until clear.

4. Add garlic and proceed to sauté for one more moment.

5. Add remaining ingredients aside from kale and cilantro. Heat to the point of boiling on high warmth. When it reaches boiling point, lessen warmth to medium-low and stew for 10 minutes, revealed. Add kale and cook for 5 additional minutes.

6. Add cilantro, salt, and pepper.

Serves 4

Serving Suggestions: Serve with Romaine and Avocado Salad

25. Super Energy Kale Soup

This fast and simple adaptation of potato kale soup has additional vegetables for more flavor and sustenance and sets aside little effort to prepare.

Prep and Cook Time: Prep and cooking time: 40 minutes

Ingredients:

- 1 medium onion, chopped
- 4 cloves garlic, chopped
- 5 cups chicken or vegetable stock
- 1 medium carrot, diced into 1/4-inch solid shapes (around 1 cup)
- 1 cup diced celery
- 2 red potatoes, diced into 1/2-inch solid shapes
- 3 cups kale, rinsed, stems eliminated and chopped exceptionally fine
- 2 tsp dried thyme

- 2 tsp dried sage

- salt and pepper to taste

Bearings:

Slash garlic and onions and let sit for 5 minutes to draw out their shrouded medical advantages.

Warmth 1 TBS stock in a medium soup pot.

Healthy Sauté onion in stock over medium warmth for around 5 minutes blending now and again.

Add garlic and proceed to sauté for one more moment.

Add stock, carrots, and celery and heat to the point of boiling on high warmth.

When it reaches boiling point, decrease warmth to a stew and keep on cooking for an additional 5 minutes. Add potatoes and cook until tender, around 15 additional minutes.

Warmth 1 TBS stock in a medium soup pot.

Healthy Sauté onion in stock over medium warmth for around 5 minutes, blending much of the time.

Add garlic and proceed to sauté for one more moment.

Add stock, carrots, and celery and heat to the point of boiling on high warmth.

When it reaches boiling point, lessen warmth to a stew and keep on cooking for an additional 5 minutes. Add potatoes and cook until tender, around 15 additional minutes.

Add kale and the rest of the ingredients and cook an additional 5 minutes. If you need to stew for a more extended time for additional flavor and extravagance, you may have to add somewhat more stock.

26. Turkey And Vegetable Chili Verde

Cruciferous vegetables, similar to kale, are probably the most wellbeing advancing vegetables around. This kale and turkey blend makes for an exceptional variant of chili that makes certain to get one of your #1 Healthiest Way of Eating plans.

Prep and Cook Time: 30 minutes

Ingredients:

- 1 medium onion, chopped
- 3 medium cloves garlic, chopped
- 1 lb ground turkey
- 1 4 oz can dice green chili
- 1 15 oz jar of diced tomatoes
- 1 TBS + 4 cups chicken stock
- 4 cups finely chopped kale

- 2 cups or 1 15 oz can (sans BPA) pinto beans, depleted and rinsed

- 2 TBS chopped new oregano

- 3 TBS chopped new cilantro

- salt and dark pepper to taste

Directions:

Slash garlic and onion and let sit for in any event 5 minutes to improve their wellbeing advancing benefits.

Warmth 1 TBS stock in a medium soup pot. Healthy Sauté onion in stock for 5 minutes over medium warmth, blending habitually. Add garlic and ground turkey with a touch of salt and pepper. Proceed to sauté, separating turkey for an additional 5 minutes.

Add diced tomatoes, chili, and stock to turkey combination and heat to the point of boiling on high warmth. Mix in chopped kale, decrease warmth to medium, and stew for an additional 10 minutes.

Add beans, stew for an additional few minutes and add herbs, salt, and pepper.

27. Zesty Mexican Soup

This zesty vegetable soup is brimming with flavor, and simple to prepare, and is the ideal expansion to your Healthiest Way of Eating. It's an extraordinary method to consolidate an assortment of vegetables into one supper, and it improves with time.

Prep and Cook Time: 40 minutes

Ingredients:

- 1 medium onion, minced
- 4 medium cloves garlic, chopped
- 2 TBS red chili powder
- 3 cups + 1 TBS chicken or vegetable stock
- 1 little to medium green ringer pepper, diced into 1/4-inch pieces
- 1 little zucchini, diced into 1/4-inch pieces
- 1 cup finely chopped collard greens
- 1 15 oz can (BPA free) diced tomatoes

- 2 cups or 1 15 oz can (BPA free) dark beans, rinsed

- 1 cup frozen yellow corn

- 1 4 oz can (BPA free) diced green chili

- 1 tsp dried oregano

- 1 tsp ground cumin

- 1/4 cup chopped pumpkin seeds

- 1/2 cup chopped new cilantro

- salt and pepper to taste

Directions:

1. Warmth 1 TBS stock in a medium soup pot. Healthy Sauté onion, garlic, and green peppers in stock over medium warmth for around 5 minutes, mixing frequently.

2. Add red chili powder and blend in well. Add stock and tomatoes. Cook for an additional 5 minutes and add beans, corn, green chili, oregano, and cumin.

3. Heat to the point of boiling on high warmth. When it starts to bubble, lessen warmth to medium-low and stew revealed for 10 minutes longer. (Stewing revealed improves the flavor.)

4. Add zucchini and collard greens and cook for 5 additional minutes. Add chopped cilantro, pumpkin seeds, salt, and pepper.

Serves 6

Serve with Romaine and Avocado Salad

CHAPTER 6
FISH

28.   5-Minute "Quick Broiled" Salmon

This is a great way to prepare Salmon that seals in its wonderful juices, brings out its best flavor and retains its moisture. It is not necessary to turn the Salmon over as it cook from both sides simultaneously.

Prep and Cook Time: 5 minutes

Ingredients:

- 1 lb Salmon fillets, with skin, cut into 2 pieces
- 2 tsp + 1 TBS fresh lemon juice
- Sea salt and pepper to taste
- 2 TBS extra virgin olive oil
- 1 medium clove garlic

- *For skinless Salmon, reduce cooking time by 1-2 minutes.

Directions:

Preheat the broiler on high and place an all stainless steel skillet (be sure the handle is also stainless steel) or cast iron pan under the heat for about 10 minutes to get it very hot. The pan should be 5-7 inches from the heat.

While the pan is heating, press or finely chop garlic and let it sit for 5 minutes.

Rub salmon with 2 tsp fresh lemon juice, salt, and pepper.

Using a hot pad, pull pan away from heat and place Salmon on hot pan, skin side down. Return to broiler. Keep in mind that it is cooking rapidly on both sides so it will be done very quickly, usually in 5 minutes, depending on thickness.

Test with a fork for doneness. It will flake easily when it is cooked. Salmon is best when it is still pink inside. The skn will peel right off after cooking.

Dress with olive oil, 1 TBS lemon juice, garlic, and salt and pepper.

29.   5-Minute Boiled Large Shrimp

Boiling Shrimp is quick and easy, and you can use boiled Shrimp in a variety of different recipes. (Taken from page 639 of the new World's Healthiest Foods book.)

Prep and Cook Time: 5 minutes

Ingredients:

- 1/2 lb large Shrimp
- 3 TBS + 1 tsp fresh lemon juice
- 3 TBS extra virgin olive oil
- 1 clove garlic
- sea salt and pepper to taste

Directions:

Press or finely chop garlic and let sit for at least 5 minutes.

Use a 3-quart saucepan filled halfway with water. Add salt to taste and 3 TBS lemon juice to the water and bring to a boil.

Peel and devein Shrimp.

When water is at a full boil, place Shrimp into the pan. Be extremely careful to avoid burning yourself when adding the Shrimp to the boiling water. Stir briefly, remove the pan from the heat and cover with a tight fitting lid. Steep small Shrimp for 1 minute, medium Shrimp for 3 minutes, and large Shrimp for 5 minutes. Cooked Shrimp look pink and are firm and opaque in the center. If the center is still translucent, steep for an addition 30 seconds covered. Remove Shrimp with a slotted spoon.

Dress with extra virgin olive oil, remaining lemon juice, garlic, salt, and pepper.

30. Baked Salmon & Walnut Patties With Red Bell Pepper Sauce

This is a simple, nutritious dish that is extra delicious served with red pepper sauce. It is one of those dishes that is so satisfying, especially when you don't have time to cook. The red pepper sauce will exceed your need for this dish. However, it will store for several days in the refrigerator and can be used on many dishes. You will enjoy having this as a staple condiment in your refrigerator.

Prep and Cook Time: 30 minutes

Ingredients:

- 1 6½ oz can of sockeye salmon, drained
- 1/4 cup chopped walnuts
- ½ cup finely minced onion
- 2 clove garlic, pressed
- ½ cup crushed whole-grain cracker
- 1 egg white
- 1 tsp prepared Dijon mustard

- ½ cup chicken or vegetable broth
- 1 TBS chopped fresh parsley
- salt & pepper to taste

Red Pepper Sauce:

- 2 red bell peppers cut in about 1 inch pieces
- ½ large onion, chopped
- 4 cloves garlic, chopped
- ½ cup vegetable stock
- 3 TBS balsamic vinegar
- 2 TBS ground walnuts
- pinch of red pepper flakes
- salt & pepper to taste

Directions:

Chop pepper, onion, garlic and Healthy Sauté in a medium sauté pan over medium-low heat for about 5 minutes, stirring frequently. Add stock and cook covered until tender, about 5 minutes. Add balsamic vinegar and red pepper flakes right before removing from heat.

1. Chop pepper, onion, garlic and Healthy Sauté in a medium sauté pan over medium-low heat for about 5 minutes, stirring frequently. Add stock and cook covered until tender, about 5 minutes. Add balsamic vinegar and red pepper flakes right before removing from heat.

Blend peppers and onions with the rest of the ingredients.

Preheat broiler on low. Combine all salmon ingredients and form into 4 patties.

Place under broiler in a baking dish, and cook for about 5 minutes on each side. Serve with sauce.

Serves 4

For optimum flavor and nutrition, serve with Sautéed Greens

31. Halibut With Ginger And Scallions

This is one of my favorite Healthiest Way of Eating recipes. The health-promoting omega-3 fatty acids from the halibut help to reduce inflammation, and the shiitake mushrooms not only enhance the flavor of this recipe but also builds a strong immune system.

Prep and Cook Time: 20 Minutes

Ingredients:

- 3/4 lb halibut cut into 2 pieces
- 1/4 cups light vegetable broth
- 1/4 cup mirin rice wine*
- 3 medium cloves garlic, chopped
- 1 TBS soy sauce
- 1 TBS fresh lemon juice
- 1 TBS minced fresh ginger
- 2 cups fresh shitake mushrooms, sliced 1/4-inch thick

- 1 cup coarsely chopped scallion

- salt and white pepper to taste

- *mirin is a sweet Japanese rice wine without the alcohol content; you can find it in many of your local health food stores or the Japanese section of your local grocery store.

Directions:

Chop garlic and let sit for 5 minutes to enhance their health-promoting properties.

Bring the broth and mirin wine to a simmer on medium-high heat in a 10-inch skillet.

Add garlic, soy sauce, lemon juice, ginger, scallions, and mushrooms.

Place halibut steaks on top, reduce heat to low and cover. Cook for about 5 minutes, depending on thickness (5 minutes for every 1/2" of thickness). Season with salt and pepper. Remove steaks and place on a plate. Spoon scallions and mushroom broth over fish and serve.

32. Miso Salmon

Try this Asian-flavored dish that is sure to become one of your favorite additions to your Healthiest Way of Eating. The salmon provides one of the best sources of those hard-to-find health-promoting omega-3 fatty acids. Enjoy!

Prep and Cook Time: 30 Minutes

Ingredients:

- 1 lb salmon, cut into 4 pieces, skin and bones removed
- 2 tsp light miso
- 1 TBS prepared Dijon mustard
- 2 TBS mirin (Japanese rice cooking wine found in the Asian section of the market)
- 4 dried medium size pieces of wakame seaweed, rinsed and soaked in 1/2 cup hot water for about 10 minutes (save water)
- 1 medium onion, cut in half and sliced
- 3 cups sliced fresh shiitake mushrooms

- 3 medium cloves garlic, chopped

- 1/2 TBS minced fresh ginger

- 2 tsp soy sauce

- salt and white pepper to taste

- garnish with minced green onion

Directions:

Preheat broiler with rack in the middle of the oven. Place a stainless steel or cast-iron skillet big enough to hold salmon under heat to get scorching (about 10 minutes).

Rinse and soak seaweed, saving the water.

Slice onion and chop garlic and let sit for 5 minutes to enhance their health-promoting properties.

Prepare glaze by mixing miso, Dijon mustard, and mirin along with a pinch of white pepper. Generously coat salmon with mixture and let set while preparing rest of ingredients.

Heat 1 TBS seaweed water in a stainless steel skillet. Healthy Sauté onion, garlic, ginger, and mushrooms in broth over medium heat for about 5 minutes. Add chopped seaweed, 1/2 cup seaweed water and soy sauce and cook for another 5 minutes. Season with salt and pepper.

Remove pan that was heating from broiler and place salmon in it. Return to broiler and cook without turning for about 3-5 minutes depending on thickness of salmon. Top with sautéed onion/mushroom mixture and minced scallion.

33.   Salmon With Dill Sauce

A classic dish that offers great taste in addition to nutrition. It's light enough for summer yet will provide you with a refreshing option for a wintertime meal. And it provides more than 30% daily value for omega-3 fatty acids, protein, selenium, and niacin. We are such fans of this recipe that we've included in Day 1 of our Healthiest Way of Eating Plan.

Prep and Cook Time: 15 minutes

Ingredients:

- 1/3 lb salmon fillet, cut in half
- 2 tsp lemon juice
- sea salt and black pepper to taste
- Dill Sauce
- 4 oz cup low-fat plain yogurt
- 1 medium cucumber, seeded and diced
- 1 TBS dill weed

- 1 tsp fresh mint

- black pepper to taste

Directions:

Quick Broil Salmon

To Quick Broil, preheat broiler on high and place an all stainless steel skillet (be sure the handle is also stainless steel) or cast iron pan under the heat for about 10 minutes to get it very hot. The pan should be 5 to 7 inches from the heat source.

Rub salmon with fresh lemon juice, salt and pepper. (You can Quick Broil with the skin on; it just takes a minute or two longer. The skin will peel right off after cooking.)

Using a hot pad, pull pan away from heat and place salmon on hot pan, skin side down. Return to broiler. Keep in mind that it is cooking rapidly on both sides so it will be done very quickly, usually in 7 minutes depending on thickness. Test with a fork for doneness. It will flake easily when it is cooked. Salmon is best when it is still pink inside.

Dill Sauce

Combine all ingredients and serve on chilled Quick Broil Salmon.

34.   Salmon With Maple Dijon Glaze

Add a tasty twist to our "Quick Broiled" Salmon with this easy-to-prepare glaze.

Prep and Cook Time: 15 minutes

Ingredients:

- 1 lb salmon fillets, with skin, cut into 3 pieces
- 2 tsp + 1 TBS fresh lemon juice
- Sea salt and pepper to taste
- Glaze:
- 1 TBS dijon mustard
- 1 tsp maple syrup
- For skinless salmon, reduce cooking time by 1-2 minutes.

Directions:

Preheat the broiler on high and place an all stainless steel skillet (be sure the handle is also stainless steel) or cast iron pan under the heat for about 10 minutes to get it very hot. The pan should be 5-7 inches from the heat source.

Rub salmon with 2 tsp lemon juice, salt, and pepper.

While the pan is heating, whisk together the glaze ingredients.

Using a hot pad, pull pan away from heat and place salmon on a hot pan, skin side down. Return to broiler. Keep in mind that it is cooking rapidly on both sides to be done very quickly.

When salmon has been cooking for 2 minutes, carefully remove from broiler, spread glaze on salmon, and return to broiler for the last 3 minutes of cooking time (or more depending on thickness).

Test with a fork for doneness. It will flake easily when it is cooked. Salmon is best when it is still pink inside. The skin will peel right off after cooking.

CHAPTER 7
CHICKEN AND TURKEY

35. Broiled Rosemary Chicken Over Puréed Lentils And Swiss Chard

This is a complete meal that is highly nutritious and delicious. It is a great meal to prepare when you have company and want to make something special.

Prep and Cook Time: 35 minutes

Ingredients:

- 3 boneless chicken breasts (6 oz each)

- 2 cups or 1 15 oz can (BPA free) lentils, drained

- 1 bunch Swiss chard

- 1 medium -sized onion, chopped

- 3 cloves garlic, pressed or finely chopped

- 1-1/2 cups crimini mushrooms, sliced
- 3 TBS vegetable or chicken broth
- 1/2 tsp dried thyme
- 1/2 tsp dried sage
- 1/2 cup walnuts
- 1 TBS + 3 TBS fresh lemon juice
- 1-1/2 TBS chopped fresh rosemary (or 2 tsp dried)
- 2 cloves pressed garlic
- 2 TBS + 1 TBS olive oil
- salt and pepper to taste

Directions:

Preheat the broiler on high and place an all stainless steel skillet (be sure the handle is also stainless steel) or cast iron pan about 6 inches from the heat for about 10 minutes to get it very hot.

While the pan is heating, rinse and pat the chicken dry and season with lemon juice, salt, and pepper.

Leaving the skin on, place the breast skin side up on the hot pan and return it to the oven. It is not necessary to turn the breast because it is cooking on both sides at once. Depending on the size, it should be cooked in about 7 minutes. Remove the skin before serving; it is left on to keep it moist while broiling. The breast is done when it is moist, yet its liquid runs clear when pierced. The inside temperature needs to reach 165 degrees Fahrenheit (74° Celcius).

While the chicken is broiling, bring a pot of water large enough to cook the chard to a boil.

Chop chard.

Chop onion, garlic, mushrooms, thyme, and sage and then Healthy Sauté them in a medium sauté pan over medium-low heat for just about 5 minutes, stirring frequently. Add lentils, walnuts and 3 TBS broth and heat through.

Purée mixture in blender or food processor with salt and pepper to taste. You will have to scrape the sides of the blender with a rubber spatula a few times.

When the water has come to a boil, add chard and boil for 3 minutes.

Drain the chard and toss with 2 TBS olive oil and 1 TBS lemon juice and salt and pepper to taste.

Place 3 TBS lemon juice, pressed garlic, chopped rosemary, salt, and pepper in a small sauté pan and heat on the stove for a minute. Turn off heat and whisk in 1 TBS olive oil.

Remove skin from chicken, slice into thirds, and serve with puréed lentils and chard. Drizzle rosemary lemon broth over chicken and lentils. Serve.

36. Curried Chicken Over Spinach

This is a great tasting dish that requires little work. The curry coconut complements the flavor of spinach, and you can easily include more vegetables. Just increase the amount of sauce slightly and add along with the bell peppers.

Prep and Cook Time: 30 minutes

Ingredients:

- 3 boneless, skinless chicken breasts cut into bite-sized pieces (6oz each)
- 1 1/2 cup chicken stock
- 3 cloves garlic, sliced
- 1 TBS fresh ginger chopped, or 1/2 tsp dried
- 1/2 tsp turmeric
- 1 tsp curry powder
- 1 medium-sized onion, cut in half and sliced
- 1 medium-sized red bell pepper julienne about 1 inch long

- 1/2 cup coconut milk, make sure it is mixed well before using

- 4 bunches of fresh spinach

- salt & white pepper to taste

Directions:

Bring water to a boil for spinach. While water is coming to a boil, cut chicken into bite-sized pieces. Healthy Sauté onion in a medium sautés pan over medium-low heat for about 5 minutes, stirring frequently. Add garlic and fresh ginger and continue to sauté for another minute. Add turmeric, and curry and mix well. Add stock, chicken, and coconut milk. Simmer for 5 minutes and add bell peppers and other vegetables you desire. Cook until chicken is done, about another 5 minutes.

While chicken is cooking, cut ends off the bunch of spinach all at once. Don't bother trying to do it one stem at a time. It will take you too long, and it is not necessary. Rinse spinach well and drop into boiling water for just 1 minute. Strain and press dry. Season with salt and pepper.

Place spinach on plates and top with chicken mixture.

Serves 4

For optimum flavor and nutrition, serve with Minted Carrots

37. Healthy Sautéed Red Cabbage With Baked Chicken Breast

This is a delicious twist on the normal red cabbage dishes. Served with our flavorful Basil Sauce, it gives it an excellent lift.

Prep and Cook Time: 30 minutes

Ingredients:

- 4 boneless, skinless chicken breasts
- 2 TBS fresh lemon juice
- 1 tsp dried rosemary
- 5 TBS broth or water
- 4 cups red cabbage chopped
- ½ cup chopped onion
- ½ cup coarsely chopped walnuts
- salt & pepper to taste
- Basil Sauce

- 4 TBS lemon juice
- 1 clove pressed garlic
- 2 TBS chopped fresh parsley
- 3 TBS chopped fresh basil
- ½ tsp salt
- ½ tsp pepper
- 3 TBS olive oil

Directions:

Preheat oven to 375. Cut chicken breasts into thirds, so they bake in a short amount of time. Rub breast pieces with 1 TBS of lemon juice, rosemary, a little salt and pepper. Place in a baking dish, and bake for about 20 minutes, covered, or until done.

In a large sauté pan, bring water or broth until the liquid starts to steam. Add onion and place cabbage on top and sprinkle cabbage with lemon juice. Cover and cook over medium heat for about 5 minutes, or until cabbage is tender.

While cabbage is cooking, mix all Basil Sauce ingredients, whisking in olive oil a little at a time in the end.

Toss cabbage with basil sauce, walnuts, salt and pepper. Serve with baked chicken breast.

Serves 4

For optimum flavor and nutrition, serve with Steamed Butternut Squash with Almond Sauce

38. Holiday Turkey With Rice Stuffing & Gravy With Fresh Herbs

Holidays are usually the time we throw caution to the wind when it comes to what we eat. But you can enjoy the holidays without compromising health with our Healthy Holiday menu, which has less fat and fewer calories—one-third fewer calories!

Ingredients:

Please read the entire recipe before shopping or beginning.

- 12-15 lb fresh organic or free-range turkey (do not use self-basting turkey)
- Stuffing:
- 1/2 cup wild rice
- 1 cup long-grain brown rice
- 1 medium onion, chopped
- 3/4 cup diced celery, about 1/4-inch pieces
- 2 cups sliced crimini mushrooms
- 1 medium green apple, diced about 1/4 inch pieces

- 4 medium cloves garlic, minced
- 1/2 cup chopped walnuts
- 6 dried apricots, coarsely chopped
- 1/2 cup raisins
- 1/2 cup chopped fresh parsley
- 2 TBS chopped fresh sage (or 2 tsp dried sage)
- 3 TBS chopped fresh thyme (or 1 TBS dried thyme)
- 1/2 TBS fennel seeds
- 1/2 cup + 1 TBS chicken broth
- salt and black pepper to taste
- Optional: cook liver for 10 minutes with gravy ingredients, remove from heat, chop and add to the stuffing mixture.

Gravy:

- 6 cups chicken broth
- 2 large carrots, chopped into large pieces
- 2 medium onions, cut into large pieces

- 2 celery sticks, cut into large pieces

- neck, wing tips and giblets from turkey (Optional: include liver and cook for about 10 minutes, remove, chop, and add to dressing ingredients)

- 1/3 cup flour mixed with water

- 1 TBS chopped fresh rosemary (or 1 tsp dried rosemary)

- 2 TBS chopped fresh thyme (or 2 tsp dried thyme)

- salt and black pepper

- *optional 1/4 cup dried porcini mushrooms

Serves: minimum of 8

Directions: Stuffing:

Bring 3-1/2 cups of lightly salted water to a boil. While water is coming to a boil, rinse the wild rice under running water in a strainer. When water is boiling, add both wild and brown rice, cover, turn heat to low and cook for about 45 minutes, until tender. Do not overcook. You will most likely have excess water when rice is cooked properly. Put cooked rice in a strainer and drain out excess water. Set aside in a large enough bowl to mix everything.

Heat 1 TBS chicken broth in a large stainless steel skillet. Healthy Sauté onion in broth over medium heat for 5 minutes. Add mushrooms and celery and continue to sauté for another 2-3 minutes.

Mix all the stuffing ingredients in a bowl and season with salt and pepper.

Always stuff the turkey just before roasting—never ahead of time—to avoid harmful bacteria's growth. Have the stuffing hot and pack it loosely in the body cavity.

Turkey:

Rinse turkey well inside and out. Pat dry. (If you had to buy a frozen turkey, make sure it is completely thawed.)

Preheat your oven to 350°F (177°C) and put the oven rack on the bottom shelf. Right before roasting the turkey, stuff it loosely with the stuffing.

Cut about 48 inches of heavy kitchen twine. Truss the turkey by first binding the legs together with the center of the length of twine. Run the twine along the turkey's sides toward the neck, tightly holding the wings to its sides with the twine. Cross the twine around the neck end of the bird and back to the legs. Loop around legs and tie a knot. Rub the turkey with a little salt and pepper.

Place turkey breast side down on a flat or V-shaped rack in a roasting pan. Make sure you use a rack inside the roasting pan. Otherwise, the skin may stick to the pan and tear. Add a cup of chicken broth to the bottom of the pan. Roast breast side down, basting about every 30 minutes with the pan juices for about 2-1/2 hours for a 12-15 lb turkey.

Bring turkey to the top of the stove, turn it to its back and remove the trussing twine. This will now allow the inside of the legs to brown along with the rest of the turkey. Baste again, and return to the oven. But first, check the breast for doneness by inserting an instant reading thermometer at the thickest part of the breast toward the neck. This will give you an idea of how much longer the turkey will need to cook. It should read about 125°F (52°C) at this point.

When the thermometer reads between 165°F and 170°F (74-77°C) in the thickest part of the thigh, the turkey is correctly done. Check the stuffing by inserting the thermometer into the center of the cavity. The stuffing should read 165°F (74°C) to be done. If it has not reached this temperature, you will have to remove it from the turkey and finish cooking it in a baking pan on its own.

It's important the stuffing reaches this temperature to be safe to eat. Check the thighs for doneness. Remove your turkey to a platter, but don't carve it for at least 20 minutes.

Gravy:

Simmer all the ingredients except oat flour, thyme, rosemary, salt, and pepper for about 1 hour on medium heat.

Strain and discard solids. Heat 1/4 cup broth in a stainless steel skillet. Whisk in flour a little at a time to incorporate. Using a wire whisk, add the rest of the broth a little at a time on low heat. Keep whisking to avoid lumps until all the liquid is incorporated.

Add rosemary and cook for another 20 minutes on low heat, stirring occasionally. Season with chopped thyme, salt, and pepper.

39. Quick Broiled Chicken Breast With Honey-Mustard Sauce

Enhance the chicken flavor with this special honey-mustard sauce and serve with spinach for a great tasting addition to your Healthiest Way of Eating. Enjoy!

Quick Broiled Chicken Breast with Honey-Mustard Sauce   Prep and Cook Time: 30 minutes

Ingredients:

- 4 boneless chicken breasts with skin
- 2+1 TBS fresh lemon juice
- 1 1/2 cups chicken broth
- 2 1/2 TBS honey
- 2 TBS Dijon mustard
- 1/4 cup sliced dried apricots
- 2 TBS coarsely chopped walnuts
- 1 TBS chopped parsley
- salt and pepper to taste

Directions:

Quick Broiled Chicken

Preheat the broiler on high and place an all stainless steel skillet (be sure the handle is also stainless steel) or cast iron pan about 6 inches from the heat for about 10 minutes to get it very hot.

While the pan is heating, rinse and pat the chicken dry and season with 2 TBS lemon juice, salt, and pepper.

Leaving the skin on, place the breast skin side up on the hot pan. It is not necessary to turn the breast because it is cooking on both sides at once. Depending on the size, it should be cooked in about 7 minutes. Begin preparing the sauce while the chicken is cooking.

The breast is done when it is moist, yet its liquid runs clear when pierced. The inside temperature needs to reach 165°F (74°C). Remove the skin before serving; it is left on to keep it moist while broiling.

Honey-Mustard Sauce

For the honey-mustard sauce, combine broth, 1 TBS lemon juice, honey, and mustard in a small saucepan. Whisk together and bring to a boil on high heat. Once it comes to a boil, simmer for about 20 minutes. You want it to be reduced to a little less than half the volume you start with. This will thicken and intensify the flavor.

Add apricots and cook on high for another 5 minutes. When the sauce is done, add chopped walnuts, parsley, salt, and pepper.

Serve over cooked spinach or other cooked greens.

40. Roast Turkey Breast With Chipotle Chili Sauce

One of the best things about the holidays is leftovers, so when you have leftover turkey, try serving it with this delicious, tangy sauce.

Prep and Cook Time: 20 minutes

Ingredients:

- Sliced Turkey Breast

- Sauce:

- 1 medium onion, finely minced

- 4 medium cloves garlic, finely minced

- 1-2 canned chipotle chilies, minced fine

- 3 TBS Dijon mustard

- 3 TBS tomato paste

- 3 TBS blackstrap molasses

- 1 TBS + 1 1/2 cup chicken broth

- 1 TBS chopped fresh oregano (or 1 tsp dried oregano)
- salt to taste

Directions:

Mince onion and garlic and let sit for 5 minutes to bring out their hidden health benefits.

Heat 1 TBS broth in a stainless steel skillet over medium heat. Healthy Sauté onion in broth for 5 minutes, stirring frequently.

Add garlic and continue to sauté for another minute.

Add rest of the ingredients and simmer for about 15 minutes, letting sauce thicken slightly.

Slice turkey and serve with sauce. (For a smoother consistency sauce, you can strain before serving.)

41. Sesame Braised Chicken & Cabbage

This highly nutritious chicken, cabbage, and kale dish is easily made and is very fresh tasting. It is a meal in one dish that is very satisfying and delicious with the chicken. By using our Healthy Sauté and stovetop braising techniques, you get a healthier dish without heated oils that are still full of flavor.

Prep and Cook Time: 30 minutes

Ingredients:

- 2 boneless skinless chicken breasts, cut into 1 inch pieces
- 4 cups green cabbage, sliced thin
- 4 cups finely chopped kale, stems removed
- 1 medium-sized onion, cut in half and sliced thin
- 1 TBS minced fresh ginger
- 2 medium cloves garlic, minced
- 1/2 cup + 1 TBS chicken broth

- 1 tsp turmeric powder

- 1 tsp ground coriander

- 1 15 oz can diced tomatoes, drained

- 2 TBS rice vinegar

- 1 TBS extra virgin olive oil

- 1/4 cup chopped scallion tops

- 1 TBS sesame seeds

- salt and white pepper to taste

Directions:

Prepare ingredients as listed above.

Heat 1 TBS broth in a stainless steel wok or large skillet. Healthy Sauté onion in broth over medium heat for about 5 minutes, frequently stirring, until translucent. Add garlic and ginger and continue to sauté for another minute.

Add chicken pieces and cook for a couple of minutes. Add turmeric, coriander, and mix with chicken. Add kale. Sauté for another couple of minutes, stirring constantly.

Add 1/2 cup broth and bring to a boil on high heat. Reduce heat and simmer over low heat covered for about 3 minutes, stirring occasionally.

Add cabbage, diced tomatoes, and vinegar and simmer for another 4 minutes. Remove from heat, toss with olive oil, salt, and pepper.

Serve sprinkled with minced scallion tops and sesame seeds.

Serves 4

Serve with Seaweed Rice

CHAPTER 8
LEAN MEAT

42. Roast Leg Of Lamb

Prep and Cook Time: Prep time: 15 minutes Cooking time: 45 minutes

Ingredients:

- butt half of boneless leg of lamb, about 3 to 4 lbs
- 8 cloves of garlic, pressed
- 3 TBS chopped rosemary
- 1/4 cup fresh lemon juice
- 2 tsp salt
- 1 tsp fresh ground pepper
- 3 carrots, peeled and sliced
- 2 onions, quartered
- 1 1/2 cups chopped celery

Directions:

Cut off excess fat from the leg of lamb. Lay leg of lamb out flat in glass baking dish. Press garlic and chop rosemary. Rub the leg with both, making sure you get it into the crevices. Pour fresh lemon juice over the lamb and sprinkle with salt. Cover and refrigerate overnight.

Preheat the oven to 425°F (218°C). Cut vegetables and place around lamb in baking dish. Sprinkle with pepper. Roast lamb and vegetables for about 15 minutes, then turn the heat down to 350°F (177°C).

After about 20 minutes, check the internal temperature of the lamb with an instant reading meat thermometer. Continue to check in the thickest part of the leg every 5 minutes until internal temperature reaches 130°F (55°C) for medium-rare. Let it rest for a few minutes before carving. Serve with vegetables and pan juices.

If vegetables are not yet tender, pour them into a pan with juice and simmer, covered over medium heat while the lamb rests.

43. Rosemary "Quick Broiled" Lamb

If you have extra time, marinating Lamb will give it great flavor. this easy preparation seals in the juices, and the skillet requires no oil. (Taken from page 737 of the 2nd Edition of the World's Healthiest Foods book.)

Rosemary Prep and Cook Time: 10 minutes

Ingredients:

- 4 lamb chops

- Marinade:

- 5 medium cloves garlic

- 3 TBS fresh lemon juice

- 2 TBS fresh rosemary, removed from stem and chopped

- Sea salt and pepper to taste

Directions:

Press garlic and let sit for 5 minutes.

Combine the marinade ingredients and Lamb chops in a bowl or plastic bag with a seal. Marinate in refrigerator 2 hours to overnight. If you don't have time to marinate, let the Lamb chops sit in the marinate for at least 10 minutes in the refrigerator.

Preheat the broiler on high and place an all stainless steel skillet (be sure the handle is also stainless steel) or cast iron pan under the heat for about 10 minutes to get it very hot. The pan should be about 5-7 inches from the heat source.

Remove Lamb chops from marinade. Using a hot pad, pull the pan out from the broiler, place the Lamb chops on the pan and return to the broiler. They cook very quickly as they are cooking on both sides simultaneously. Do not turn.

Broil for 7-10 minutes for medium-rare, depending on the thickness of the chops. They are done when the internal temperature is 135°F (57°C). For medium-well chops, cook 2-3 minutes longer.

CHAPTER 9
VEGETARIAN ENTREES

44. Indian-Style Lentils

Combine this tasty lentil dish with rice for a hearty meatless meal to add to your Healthiest Way of Eating. It will provide you with a complete protein as well many other health-promoting nutrients.

Prep and Cook Time: 20 minutes

Ingredients:

- 1 medium-size onion, diced
- 1 TBS vegetable broth
- 2 cloves garlic, minced
- 1 tsp ginger
- 1/2 tsp turmeric
- 1/2 tsp salt

- 1 cup canned diced tomatoes

- 2 cups or 1 15-oz can (BPA free) lentils

- 1 cup frozen spinach

Directions:

Dice onions and mince garlic and sit for at least 5 minutes to bring out their health-promoting properties.

Healthy sauté onion in 1 TBS broth for 3 minutes.

Add garlic, ginger, turmeric, salt, tomatoes and lentils.

Simmer covered for 5-7 minutes.

Add 1 cup of frozen spinach and continue simmering for 2 more minutes.

Serves 2

Serve over brown rice.

45. Quick Black Bean Chili

Chili is enjoyed even during the summer months, and this rich, hearty and flavorful version can be prepared in less than 30 minutes!

Prep and Cook Time: 30 minutes

Ingredients:

- 1 medium onion, chopped
- 2 cloves garlic, minced or pressed
- 2 cups or 1 15 oz can (BPA-free) black beans
- 1 15 oz can diced tomatoes
- 1 TBS chili powder
- 1/2 cup cilantro

Directions:

Chop onions and mince or press garlic and sit for at least 5 minutes to enhance their health-promoting properties.

Place all ingredients—except cilantro—in a pot, cover, and let simmer for about 20 minutes.

Top with cilantro and serve.

CHAPTER 10
SIDE SALAD/DRESSINGS

46.   Great Antipasto Salad

It's great to have a salad on hand to enjoy as part of your Healthiest Way of Eating. And this one actually gets better with time; it will keep in the refrigerator for one week. It's also an excellent source of health-promoting health vitamin A; one serving provides 305% of the daily value for this vital nutrient. Enjoy!

Prep and Cook Time: prep time: 15 min; marinating time: 15 min

Ingredients:

- 2 cups carrots, turned
- 1-1/2 cups thickly sliced celery
- 1 cup fresh sliced fennel bulb
- 2 TBS rinsed and quartered Kalamata olives
- 2 TBS capers, rinsed

- Dressing

- 1-1/2 tsp dried Italian mixed herbs

- 2 medium cloves garlic, pressed

- 2 tsp Dijon mustard

- 1 tsp honey

- 1/4 tsp salt

- 1/4 tsp cracked black pepper

- 1-1/2 TBS fresh lemon juice

- extra virgin olive oil to taste

Directions:

Press garlic and let sit for 5 minutes to enhance its health-promoting benefits.

Bring water to boil in a steamer and add carrots and steam for 4 minutes. Add celery and fennel and steam for just 1 more minute.

Remove from heat and place in a bowl with capers and olives.

Whisk all dressing ingredients together, drizzling olive oil at the end a little at a time.

Toss with vegetables and marinate for at least 15 minutes before serving.

47. Kiwi Salad

You can serve this dish as either a salad or dessert. It not only tastes great, but the vibrant mixture of colors is a beautiful addition to your table. Enjoy!

Prep and Cook Time: 10 minutes

Ingredients:

- 6 kiwifruit, peeled and sliced
- 1 cup sliced strawberries
- 1 cup fresh pineapple cut into 1 inch pieces
- 1 TBS lemon juice
- 1 tsp honey

Directions:

Mix all ingredients together and serve immediately.

48. Grape And Melon Salad

Take advantage of the fruits that are in season and satisfy your sweet tooth by enjoying this summer salad that takes only minutes to prepare. If you select red/purple grapes you will get the added benefit of the phytonutrient, reservatrol, which has been found to be a powerful antioxidant.

Prep and Cook Time: 15 minutes

Ingredients:

- 1 lb seedless grapes
- 1 cantaloupe, scooped out with melon baller
- 2 cups of seedless watermelon, scooped out with melon baller
- 1/2 cup whole peppermint leaves
- 2 TBS lemon juice

Directions:

Mix all ingredients together. Toss with whole peppermint leaves and refrigerate for a couple hours. Remove leaves and serve.

49. Mediterranean Tomato Salad

This easy to prepare Mediterranean-style salad complements almost any meal.

Prep and Cook Time: 5 minutes

Ingredients:

- 2 large ripe tomatoes, chopped into large pieces
- 1 medium red onion, sliced thin
- 2 cloves garlic, minced
- 1 TBS lemon juice or vinegar
- 3 TBS extra virgin olive oil
- 10 fresh basil leaves, torn into small pieces
- Sea salt and pepper to taste
- Optional:
- 1/2 cup mozzarella cheese
- 6 olives, chopped

- 2 tsp capers

- anchovies (use however much suits your palate)

Directions:

Slice onions and mince garlic and let sit for 5 minutes to bring out their health-promoting benefits.

Combine and toss all ingredients. Add salt and pepper to taste.

50. Cranberry Sauce

Cranberry sauce doesn't have to take a long time to prepare. Enjoy this delicious accompaniment to your Healthy Holiday Turkey in just minutes. You will also be gaining the benefits of its rich concentration of health-promoting vitamin C and antioxidants found in cranberries.

Prep and Cook Time: 15 minutes

Ingredients:

- 1 cup fresh orange juice
- 1 tsp minced fresh ginger
- 1 tsp minced orange zest
- 1/4 tsp cinnamon
- 12 oz bag of fresh or frozen cranberries
- 1/2 cup crushed pineapple
- 1/2 cup honey

Directions:

Bring orange juice, ginger, zest and cinnamon to a boil on high heat in a medium saucepan.

Rinse cranberries and add once liquid is boiling. Reduce heat to medium and cook uncovered for about 10 minutes.

Add crushed pineapple and honey. Remove from heat and cool.

Yields 2 cups

Serving Suggestions: Serve with

Holiday Turkey with Rice Stuffing and Herbed Gravy

CPSIA information can be obtained
at www.ICGtesting.com
Printed in the USA
BVHW092254250521
608096BV00004B/322